IMAGES
of America

EMMETT TOWNSHIP

AERIAL VIEW. This aerial view of Emmett in the early 1900s shows Our Lady of Mt. Carmel Church, the grain elevator, the train depot, Emmet House, and the Dewey Hotel. (Courtesy of the author.)

ON THE COVER: Around 1930, corn, wheat, oats, and beans were raised in abundance and shipped by train from the largest grain elevators in St. Clair County. Farmers from the townships depended on Emmett Elevator to ship their harvests. (Courtesy of Donnellon and Grace families.)

IMAGES
of America

EMMETT TOWNSHIP

Marian Brennan Pratt

ARCADIA
PUBLISHING

Published by Arcadia Publishing
Charleston, South Carolina

Library of Congress Control Number: 2012939007

For all general information, please contact Arcadia Publishing:
Telephone 843-853-2070
Fax 843-853-0044
E-mail sales@arcadiapublishing.com
For customer service and orders:
Toll-Free 1-888-313-2665

Visit us on the Internet at www.arcadiapublishing.com

I dedicate this labor of love to my good friends,
the lads and lassies of Emmett.

CONTENTS

ACKNOWLEDGMENTS

Work on this project has rekindled some interest in past generations. Rummaging through trunks and boxes for old pictures has generated memories. I thank all the good citizens of Emmett, the township and the village, for the time they spent digging up the evidence that there was life before us. I would like to thank my cousin Patti Hacht for proposing the original idea to me. There were times, Patti, when I considered taking all my accoutrements in regard to this project and placing them lovingly on your front porch. Also, thanks to Bob Weir, who went above and beyond, not only sending me pictures of the machinery but also giving me information for captions. Did I mention that he was in India at the time but had the photographs on his computer? Karen Breen-Bondi, another cousin, was very helpful with images that people in Emmett quite possibly have not seen before. Thanks to Cecelia Marko for her proofreading skills. Thanks to those who let me borrow their family photographs, trusting that they would see them again sometime. And I owe Jim Brennan a great deal for letting me use some of his information. I did not manage to drive my editor, Sandy Shalton, crazy while I ranted and raved on several occasions. When I was all done, she would say, "You can do it, Marian." And thank you to Laura Saylor, who helped me see it through to the end. In regard to picture credits, I was happy to give credit to anyone who had supplied pictures, but there were a lot of the same postcards and some gave me pictures of the same relative. If I have given the wrong person credit, please be kind; we are all cousins.

FOREWORD

The following pages have been written as honestly as any woman of Irish descent can write. I have researched actual facts and dates and have also included some, shall we say, folklore, which has been handed down so religiously that it has to be accepted as truth. Those of us who were born and raised in this little town of Emmett did not know just how much of Ireland was in each of us until we decided, as a group of about 20, to travel to the "Auld Sod." Most of us felt that we had "gone home." We met people that we resemble, or they resembled us! The Irish are said to be a very friendly people and that was proven to us over and over in our travels around the beautiful island. Hopefully, the truthfulness of my pictures, historical facts, and stories serve our heritage well, and if you happen to visit our little town today, you will find the common Irish names of Brennan, Pierce, Ryan, Crowley, Foley, and O'Connor, to name a few. They are plentiful in both the living and the dead who now reside in Our Lady of Mt. Carmel Cemetery, just a mile or two east of town.

—Elaine Coady Rawlins

INTRODUCTION

A great many of the founding fathers of Emmett were Irish Catholics. Because they were Irish, they named the area Emmett—the township and the village—after the person they considered to be a true Irish hero: Robert Emmet. His life story is romantic and heroic at best and sad and gruesome at worst.

Emmet was born in Dublin, Ireland, on March 4, 1778. Though his 1803 rebellion was a complete failure, he was still jailed, put on trial, tortured, and killed, making him a true Irish hero. He wrote a letter from his cell in Kilmainham Jail in Dublin that was addressed to "Miss Sarah Curran, the Priory, Rathfarnham," Emmet gave it to the prison warden, who he trusted, but the warden betrayed him and gave the letter to the police, nearly costing Curran her life. Emmet's friend from Trinity College, Thomas Moore, wrote very popular ballads about Emmett and Sarah:

> Oh breathe not his name! Let it sleep in the shade,
> She is far from the land where her young hero sleeps
> And lovers around her are sighing.

Emmet's "Speech From The Dock," delivered after he was convicted, is widely quoted and remembered. It has been said that Abraham Lincoln memorized the speech when he was a boy. It ultimately had an influence on others like him to fight for freedom.

> Let no man write my epitaph; for as no man who knows my motives dare now vindicate them, let not prejudice or ignorance, asperse them. Let them and me rest in obscurity and peace, and my tomb remain uninscribed, and my memory in oblivion, until other times and other men can do justice to my character. When my country takes her place among the nations of the earth, then and not till then, let my epitaph be written. I have done.

There is much mystery and speculation regarding the whereabouts of Emmet's remains, which were secretly removed from Bully's Acre in Kilmainham. It was thought that his remains were buried in Dublin's Anglican church. When the vault was inspected in the 1950s, a headless corpse was found and suspected of being Emmet's, but it could not be identified. The most plausible theory is that the remains were taken to the Church of Ireland in Dublin under cover of the burial of Robert's sister, Mary Anne Holmes, in 1804. In the 1980s, the church was turned into a nightclub and all the coffins were removed from the vaults.

There were many wars and insurrections against British rule. "A Nation Once Again" was written in hope of freedom and every Irishman, young and old, knew the words:

> When boyhood's fire was in my blood, I read of ancient freemen,
> For Greece and Rome who bravely stood, Three hundred men and three men;
> For, Freedom comes from God's right hand, And needs a Godly train;
> And righteous men must make our land A Nation once again
> So, as I grew from boy to man, My spirit of each selfish plan
> When my dear country shall be made A Nation once again!

The people who came here from Ireland were used to unrest and hostility in their everyday lives. Most left home without any clear knowledge of what life would be like for them at the end of their adventure, but they left anyway, holding on to hope. Their stamina can be likened to their own young hero, Robert Emmet, in that they too were willing to step up and take a chance for what they wanted.

The quality of life in the New World changed considerably between the 1600s and the 1800s, with the land eventually becoming friendlier. In 1836, immigrants flocking to the New World from all over Europe could make the trip inland from New York and Boston more easily because of the Erie and Weland Canals. The development of the Canadian Railway assisted those coming through Halifax and Quebec. St. Clair County was the first place immigrants saw when they crossed the St. Clair River by boat at Sarnia, Canada, and found themselves in Port Huron, Michigan. Many proceeded to Flint and Lansing but some lingered in Emmett and made it their home. Jobs could be had in lumbering camps and on railroad gangs. Also, good, rich farmland was available—better than the rocky, overworked land they were used to. Besides those commodities shipped by Emmett Elevator, hay was and continues to be important, and raising cattle for beef or milk production was significant. It has become apparent now that small family farms are diminishing and the nature of the township is changing from an agricultural to a rural residential community. Owners of small farms are finding it increasingly hard to make a living due to higher costs in maintaining their equipment, more expensive supplies and planting material, and difficulty finding good hired help.

On February 19, 1850, the land that would be called Emmett Township was taken from the township of Clyde by an act of the Michigan Legislature. The land had been owned by the Cherokee tribe and was ceded to the United States in the Treaty of Detroit in 1807. A description of the new township's location was "7 North, Range 14 East," which requires a rather complicated explanation. The description of all townships in Michigan referred to its relation to where the original north-south baseline—now 8 Mile Road in Detroit—met the east-west line, or the "principal meridian," which runs through the center of Ingrahm County. Emmett Township was the seventh township north of the baseline and the 14th township east of the principal meridian. The townships were well platted out and organized at the time, but the village was not officially created until April 21, 1883, when the name was changed to Emmett.

The townships of Emmett, Kenockee, Riley, and Wales were developed at the same time. Emmett, the primary village of the area, was located at the intersection of those four townships. The old saying goes, "Capac when you are hungry, Emmett when you are dry, Goodells when you are busted, Kenockee when you die."

The people in the townships were friendly with each other because many were Irish and some were relatives, living just down the road in another township. But if the boys from one township challenged the other three townships to a baseball tournament, all bets were off. The spirit of fierce competition was like electricity in the air over the baseball diamonds. Little boys scrambled to get a good place where they could see; after all, soon they would be old enough to play. The audience waited while the rules were being set up. The men argued back and forth, throwing their hats on the ground, and they finally agreed to what the wives said were pretty much the same rules they used the last time. And the game began.

Many Irish immigrants came to Emmett because their relatives were already here because of patriarch Patrick "Pa" Kennedy. As the story goes, Kennedy had "stolen" an education in Ireland—Catholic Irish were not allowed a formal education. Kennedy made a lot of connections in America. Not only was he the first postmaster, he also had a newspaper friend at the *Irish World* in New York (some say it was the *Boston Pilot* newspaper in Boston), and he published advertisements describing what a wonderful place Emmett was. Kennedy was also the land agent and, as such, was able to settle each new family in an area with "their own," meaning that if they were from County Kerry in Ireland, their neighbors would also be from County Kerry. The residents seemed to like this arrangement and happily settled into life as they had known it in the "Old Sod." Eventually, they became quite "clannish." There was much concern among the older ladies if a girl from the Kerry settlement should want to marry a lad from the Cork settlement, "She should know her place, after all, begorra!" They firmly held their priorities and a pecking order, much the same as Boston high society.

The Irish are strong, passionate people, with tight family ties. They loved to have parties and sing and dance and have a "bit of the bubbly" at various times. Another side of the Irish psyche is their love of competition. Stories have been told of what the men would do in Emmett bars on a summer's eve. For want of something better to do having exhausted all attempts to pick a fight with some of the other lads, they would put all their names in the hat and draw out two. That lucky pair would become the contenders for the evening's boxing entertainment. The bar owner, if he was lucky enough to realize what was going on, would order them all outside and the fight would begin.

As time passed, the spelling of Emmett or Emmet—the latter being the correct spelling of the town's namesake—appears to have been left according to the personal preference of the township clerk. Over time, it gradually switched to the "two-t" version.

Charley A. Cogley was a colorful Irish gent who always carried a bit of humor in his pocket. He believed that outside of Ireland, Emmett is the "cat's ankles." Here is a "Boost for Emmett" by Cogley from 1924:

> If you're full of prattle, ladies and crazy to stitch 'n sew
> Walk in to Jonnie Downse's 'N examine his calico.
> Jonnie keeps our dry goods. He charges no tax or fees
> So boys drop in next summer 'N buy your B.V.Ds.
> If you're down in the dumps 'n hungry, And wish you never were born,
> Indulge at Martin Brandon's 'N pay when you sell your corn.
> If you're troubled with pyorrhea, Radiant nose or gas,
> Sneak in to Dr. Haight's And smell his sassafras.
> You asked about our politics Well all we can say for that,
> Is 99 out of 110 Are 99 tenths democrat.
> So boys if you're up for sportin' or spoonin' or moonin' the same,
> Jazz up your Lizzie for Emmett, You'll be tickled stiff you came.

In 1916, the town continued to grow, with professionals, tradesman, and many businesses. On October 17, 1916, a fire swept through the business section of the village and was reported in a cover story in the *Port Huron Times-Herald*. The blaze caused an estimated loss of $80,000. All of the buildings on the west side of Main Street and all but two—the Emmet House and the post office—on the east side were destroyed. As more buildings were engulfed, it became apparent that the Emmet House would be next. The flaming debris was threatening to catch the roof on fire. Men gathered up all the linens the hotel had, soaked them with water, and threw them on the roof; they thought they could at least save something. Of the 18 structures north of the Grand Trunk railway, only five remained standing. The McCabe Bank, the newly completed opera house, and the general store all were destroyed. The fire started in the McIntyre poolroom and barbershop and spread rapidly to the south, driven by high winds. Some store owners rebuilt, but some did not, and the town would never see that kind of growth and prosperity again. It seemed as if the high winds, which carried the fire so fast, had sucked the life out of their town. Emmett never recovered.

In 1935, the township board discussed building a township hall. A half-acre of land was purchased from Dan Foley for the building site. After all the sketches were approved and the permits pulled, work began. The lot was fenced and graveled by Thomas Byrne and John Sullivan at 45¢ per hour. Sullivan received $105 for installing the foundations, $100 for the hall, and $5 for the outhouse, in addition to receiving $280 for labor. Norm Sweeney was hired to paint the inside of the hall for $95. The first meeting in the new hall was held on January 19, 1938. No mention is made in the minutes as to whether the project came in on time or if there was an official dedication, but a party was held at the hall for the township residents with food and dancing. A new township hall is in place today, but the old one lasted 63 years, a testament to the carpenters of Emmett.

When the present township hall was being built, volunteer help was used as well. Joe Francek and crew did much of the work and their labors were noted and appreciated. The new building is beautiful and it could not have been in a better place, accessible and close to town. The township dedicated the new hall in 2001.

One

OUR TOWN

MOUNT CROWLEY. This photograph shows the east side of Main Street in the village of Mount Crowley, facing south. Emmett was originally called Mount Crowley, after Thomas Crowley, one of the first settlers to the area. Crowley is said to have owned the land that the town was built upon. Village residents joked that they could not see any reason why anyone would call the place "Mount" since it was just about the flattest piece of land they had ever seen. (Courtesy of Jim and Darlene Stapleton.)

BUSINESS. Here is the west side of Main Street, facing south. Around the turn of the century, Emmett featured many new businesses, including five grocery stores, a three-story men's clothing store and boot shop, a telephone office, an ice cream parlor, a barbershop and poolroom, and several ladies' dress shops. (Courtesy of Jim and Darlene Stapleton.)

EMMET HOUSE. Emmet House was a hotel in a prime location. When a couple entered, the man would join his friends at the bar and was served beer, wine, or mixed drinks. The ladies were escorted into a front parlor and allowed one alcoholic drink only, plus tea and cakes. (Courtesy of Rosemary and Joe Ryan.)

12

DRUGSTORE. D.F. Ahearn stands in front of his establishment with an unidentified little girl. His storefront announced, "Drugs and Medicines D.F. Ahearn 1907, Emmett, Michigan." The storefront windows are unique with smaller panes of glass surrounding the large ones. (Courtesy of Jim and Darlene Stapleton.)

TRAIN DEPOT. Freight trains carried the mail but could not stop at every town. The mailbag was positioned on a hook outside the depot, and when the train blew through town, the bag was picked off the hook by a mechanism on the train. Former employee Edsel Dunn recalled that, as the outgoing mail was picked up, he had to throw the bag of incoming mail for Emmett off the moving train, hoping it hit something other than the ditch. (Courtesy of the Emmett Diner.)

MEAT MARKET. The two large showcases in Fred Brogan's meat market were very well stocked. The customer could see what he was buying and be assured that it had been kept refrigerated. The market was also stocked with a few staple items like flour and corn meal. Brogan's office was in back, where he could work and also see customers when they came into the store. (Courtesy of Rosemary Brogan Ryan.)

REID'S STORE. The *Port Huron Times Herald* wrote an article on Reid's Store, the "store that has everything." Reid's carried jars, canned goods for those who did not do fancy canning, some other grocery items, yard goods, and clothes. Notice the copper ceiling and the rocking chair for weary shoppers. (Courtesy of Genevieve Sheehey.)

OFFICE OF MICHAEL REID. This is the office of county treasurer Michael Reid. The office was quite beautiful; notice the fancy chandelier and the arched windows. The desks were made of wood and were big enough for the staff of seven to carry out the day-to-day work of the county. (Courtesy of Helen Wendling.)

HOTEL DEWEY. Hotel Dewey was located diagonally from Emmet House. Both hotels were built about the same time and had pretty much the same rules of propriety for women, making them competitors. Emmet House seems to have been the more polished of the two. (Courtesy of Emmett Diner.)

EMMETT VOLUNTEER FIRE DEPARTMENT. From left to right, the fire department included Jim Scheible, Mike Scheible, Bill Morgan, Lambert Pierce, Don Bondy, Elmer Hazelman, Bob Quain, Edward Butler, Don Kring, Edsel Dunn, Pat Grace, Jack Cowhy, Irwin Scheible, Dutch Brandon, Martin Weir, Tom Butler, Leo Cody, unidentified, Tony Ureel, Bob Morgan, Harold Densmore,

Pat Neaton, Leo Dunnigan, and Gerald Butler. Ray Butler and Dick Densmore are sitting in the fire truck. An addition was built on to the existing fire hall in 1976 and dedicated to the memory of Irwin Scheible, the first chief of the Emmett Fire Department, when it was organized in 1946. (Courtesy of Emmett Diner.)

FIRE HALL. Today, this building still houses Emmett's volunteer fire department. The fleet includes the fire engine, which carries 2,500 gallons of water, the 1,500-gallon water truck, the 100-gallon grass truck, and an emergency vehicle. (Courtesy of Jack Beleskey.)

Weir's Store. Marge Weir and her mother-in-law, Theresa, ran the store with the help of Marge's son Bob. If a woman was waiting for her husband to get an implement fixed, she could go next door to see Marge in the store and pick up some Wonder Bread, Orange Crush pop for the kids, and a cigar for her husband. She might even take advantage of that 15¢ deal. (Courtesy of Bob Weir.)

CSB BANK. The Commercial and Savings Bank (CSB) built an imposing structure on the same spot where Hotel Dewey once stood. It is still a small community bank with employees and customers knowing each other on a first-name basis. (Courtesy of the author.)

Two

Farm Implements

HAY PRESS. The writing on the side of this hay press reads, "The New Way Press No. 11526." Its main function was to press hay, nothing more. It was hand-fed and pressed the hay tight while a worker installed the wires or bale ties around the hay, thus forming a man-made bale. This crew included Dave Reeves, Dave Mahar, Fonce Mahar, Jim Malley, Frank Cowhy, Joe Mahar, Amy Kinney, Mayme Mahar Kinney, and Alfred Cowhy. (Courtesy of Emmett Diner.)

POWERFUL HORSES, 1930s. This team of hardworking horses is three lines, three abreast. Gordan Theisen, the driver, is working up the soil with the plough in preparation for planting. There are so many horses because the plough is made up of a series of plough points, which must cut deep into the soil and roll it over. (Courtesy of Emmett Diner.)

THRASHING MACHINE. Ed Butler's McCormick Dearing 1020 tractor and thrashing machine offered a pretty bumpy ride, but it was more than capable of towing the lumbering "thrasher" into the barn. All the neighbors followed the machine from farm to farm, helping each other take off their crops. The women of each household fed the "thrashers" each day. (Courtesy of Emmett Diner.)

AN INVENTION. Fonce Mahar (tentatively identified as far right, top row) and Alfred Cowhy (tentatively identified as far right, bottom row) are taking a time-out to pose for the camera, capturing this fierce-looking machine with steam rolling out of it. The others could not be identified. Later called a threshing machine, this type of implement was invented by Andrew Meikle, a Scottish mechanical engineer. (Courtesy of Emmett Diner.)

WEIR'S TRACTORS. Fred Weir and his son Martin ran an implement dealership out of this building. It was dedicated mostly to tractors, but they sold everything, and master mechanic Leo Coady could fix anything. International Harvester, McCormick-Deering, and Atlas tires were sold. They also operated a three-pump Standard Oil station. (Courtesy of Bob Weir.)

CATERPILLAR. This tractor from around 1910 featured a standard, unpadded metal seat. The "crawler" or "caterpillar" treads enable the tractor to work on soft, moist soil without getting stuck in the field. The worst thing for a farmer is having to wait to get out in the fields when there has been too much rain. (Courtesy of Bob Weir.)

REAPER. Two farmers operate this steel-wheeled tractor and a reaper in the 1920s. In those days, the tractor merely pulled the implement across the field, just as horses had done. The man on the reaper pulled levers to bring in the harvest. The first reaper was patented in 1834 by Cyrus McCormick. From that first successful invention came McCormick-Deering, Farmall, and International Harvester. (Courtesy of Bob Weir.)

FARMALL SUPER C. Martin Weir (far left) poses with employees of Fred Weir & Son farm implement dealership in front of a new Farmall Super C tractor. Next to Martin, from left to right, are Norm Dukatz and Paul Koves, with master tractor mechanic Leo Coady in the background. This photograph was professionally taken and used in promotional literature in 1953. (Courtesy of Bob Weir.)

POST OFFICE AND TRACTOR. Patrick Kennedy was the area's first postmaster but he did not get a building until 1869. He used to take mail to church with him and pass it out after mass. Part of his farm acreage is on Emmett Road and is now the property of Dorma Brennan and her late husband, Bob (on the tractor). One of their outbuildings (behind the tractor) may be the remains of that first post office. (Courtesy of Dorma Brennan.)

28

FOUR-BY-FOURS. This image shows what the modern farm has become. The Peters farming family has worked hard for a number of years to do big business with big machinery. The small figure standing in front of these behemoth tractors is Randy Peters, who runs the business with his brothers. (Courtesy of the Peters family.)

GRAIN CART. This cart replaced the gravity box. It holds approximately 1,100 bushels of grain and transports them to the truck. The combines are able to unload into the grain cart without stopping. Combines can harvest approximately 30 acres of wheat or soybeans per hour. (Courtesy of the Peters family.)

GRAVITY BOXES. Pat Quain crosses M-19 and heads down Brandon Road toward home. He is pulling two gravity boxes, although the back one did not make it into the photograph. He will load up again and be on his way back to the elevator. A gravity box is built like a cone so when the chute is opened the grain just slides right out the bottom. (Courtesy of the author.)

ANTIQUE CAR. Richard and Rita Jane Coady are ready to go on a road trip in their father's Ford Model T, made on Henry Ford's assembly lines in nearby Detroit. (Courtesy of Elaine Rawlins.)

THE MAXWELL. Bill Stapleton poses inside the Maxwell. In 1923, Maxwell Motor Company produced cars with Chalmers and Chrysler before bringing in Walter Chrysler to save their ailing company. Two years later, Chrysler cars replaced Maxwell and were thought by some to be a classy alternative to the blue-collar Ford and Chevrolet cars. (Courtesy of Jim and Darlene Stapleton.)

LUMBER WORKERS. John Purtell (middle) is pictured here with a logging crew in the northern woods of Michigan. The rest of the crew cannot be identified. Another Emmett resident, Frank Brogan, also tried his hand at lumber work, which is how he met his future wife, Mary Carol, the camp cook. Frank brought her back to Emmett and married her. (Courtesy of the author.)

LUMBER CAMP. In this photograph, the only one who can be identified, again, is John Purtell (second from right). Horses were a very necessary part of the lumber business. Thee two pictured here look fit and capable of hauling logs to the river to eventually float them to market. Christopher Brandon was another lumberman from Emmett. He made the journey to the north Michigan woods and took his wife with him. He was the camp foreman and his wife, Gertrude Klauka Brandon, was the camp cook.

32

MY HORSE, OLD JAKE. Elizabeth Gleason stands on a farm wagon with the reins of a horse in her hands. Women knew how to handle horses in farming communities like Emmett. If one of the workers was sick or a hired hand had failed to show up, farmers would head for the house to enlist the help of their wife or daughter. (Courtesy of Ray and Vickie Gleason.)

FARMERS IN THE FIELD. On a summer day in the 1940s, brothers Joe, Vin, and Dan Ryan (pictured from left to right) work a field on their parent's farm on Sheridan Road. Dan is driving a John Deere tractor with the metal wheels common at the time. Vin and Joe are working on the binder shocking wheat, getting ready for the thrashing machine and crew to arrive. Daniel Ryan and Ella Clifford Ryan were owners of property designated as a centennial farm. The house cost $600 to build. This property with the house is located across the road. (Courtesy of Joe and Rosemary Ryan.)

Three

THE CHURCH

A BAD DAY. In 1966, the fall dinner was being served when the big Gothic church burst into flames. The parishioners were horrified. Fr. John F. Farrell had retired and was living at the rectory as pastor emeritus. A photograph of him in the local newspaper showed fire trucks from all the surrounding towns pouring gallons of water on the flames. The sky turned black and the air was thick with smoke as Father Farrell stood on the lawn and watched his church burn, his head tipped back to see the steeple, which was about to fall. (Courtesy of the *Port Huron Times Herald*.)

BEGINNINGS. In 1840, the first Catholic mass was celebrated, but it was not until 1855 that a cemetery and small log church were established east of the village. That log church burned in 1865, and the parishioners erected the wood frame structure pictured in this drawing. It also shows a rectory farther east on high ground. A faint impression of the water trough line that brought water from the tank at the rectory to the church is visible. The inscription says, "August 23, 1851, until the fire in 1861," which begs to differ with the dates recorded. The drawing hangs in the cemetery chapel, which was built very close to the spot where the priest's house and barn stood so many years ago. Gene and Betty Haley were instrumental in planning the chapel. The artist was Oswald Cogley's brother. (Our Lady of Mt. Carmel Records.)

FATHER KILROY. The first priest many encountered in America was Fr. Laurence Kilroy, a circuit rider priest responsible for all of St. Clair County. He was from King's County, Ireland, and was a backbone of the early church. Many stories were told about the miracles occurring when he traveled. Once, while out on a winter night, he was stopped by a wild, howling wind, but he nudged the reins and his horses brought him through it. Somehow, his lantern lights did not blow out. (Our Lady of Mt. Carmel records.)

THE DISAGREEMENT. Ladies in early Emmett visit with neighbors out by the street. The people of Emmett were socially minded and created a community with their neighbors. When the second church at Kenockee burned in the late 1890s, it became apparent that a new, larger church building was needed. Bishop John Foley of the Catholic diocese wanted the new church built in Emmett. The Emmett people were delighted, but people from Kenockee were not. The battle was settled by Bishop Foley. In a letter, he pointed out that Emmett surely deserved a substantial edifice in which to worship. He also agreed that there were tender memories in the Kenockee church, but the church needed to be built in Emmett, where a larger concentration of people resided. The bishop was a tactful arbitrator, and the church was built in Emmett with the goodwill of all. (Our Lady of Mt. Carmel records.)

WORK BEGINS. More than 100 skilled and unskilled laborers came to Emmett to build the big Gothic church in the 1890s. The Kavanaghs, owners of the Emmet House, laid 100 mattresses on the floor of their large ballroom so the men could sleep. It was not only Detroit laborers who came to work. Word had spread that the Emmett ladies served three square meals a day, including pie and cold beer. Non-Catholic wives eventually got sick of their husbands flocking to Emmett whenever the call for workers went out. (Our Lady of Mt. Carmel records.)

WORK IS ALMOST COMPLETED. The Emmett men started by hauling loads of stone in for the foundation with teams of horses. They wagered about who would bring in the first load. Massive amounts of building supplies came in on the train and the men took their teams to the station to transport the loads to the building site. The huge stained-glass windows and the organ came by train also. The men did not exactly jump at the chance to bring that cargo in. The church was dedicated on Saturday, January 18, 1897, by Bishop Foley, who had also arrived on the train. The cost of the church and rectory was $33,767. The church used today, built in 1966, cost $570,000 and was built by contractors. It is pictured on page 54. (Our Lady of Mt. Carmel records.)

THE RECTORY. While the old church is gone, the rectory, or priest's house, at Our Lady of Mt. Carmel still stands. Since the rectory was built at the same time as the church, it has held up very well, owing partially to work done over the years. (Our Lady of Mt. Carmel records.)

MIDDLE AISLE. This is the middle aisle of the old church in Emmett, built in 1897, which has been witness to most of the weddings held in Emmett. Besides weddings, there were also baptisms, funerals, first communions, confirmations, 40 Hours Devotion, the mission, confessions, Stations of the Cross during Lent, Sunday mass, and much more. (Courtesy of Sally Lichota.)

Celebrating 125 Years

A PARISH ARTIST. For the 125th anniversary of the parish, Emmett artist Ann Donnellon was asked to draw a composite of the churches. She produced this amazing pen and ink drawing of the three churches piled on top of each other but with each easily recognizable, as part of the story of Our Lady of Mt. Carmel. Donnellon passed away in 2011. (Courtesy of the author.)

SCHOOL. When the Our Lady of Mt. Carmel School, pictured here, was first built in 1924, Immaculate Heart of Mary nuns from Monroe were hired to teach grades one through 10. Fr. John F. Farrell, upon hearing that the nuns were arriving early, moved out of the rectory and in with a parish family so the nuns could have a place to stay before the convent was finished. Father Farrell was a kind and gentle soul who wanted to see the children get a good education. Every parish child in the school was provided a free education courtesy of the parish's income.

The school operated for 32 years in the manner, but a lack of money and teachers made Father Farrell rethink his educational plans and cut the ninth and 10th grades. The thinking was that students might be better off entering high school together with their peers, making it easier to make friends. This picture of the entire school was taken in 1956 on the last day that ninth and 10th grade students attended Our Lady of Mt. Carmel School. The school continued until the new one was built in 1966. (Our Lady of Mt. Carmel records.)

THE CONVENT. This is the convent where the nuns lived. The parish has done some work on the building and it is now the parish business office. Since Our Lady of Mt. Carmel is now clustered with Sacred Heart in Yale and St. Edward in Lakeport, the office staff is in Emmett only part-time. (Courtesy of the author.)

THE DAUGHTERS OF ISABELLA. Known as the "D of I," the Daughters of Isabella is a benevolent society but is also out for a little fun. In this image, members get ready for a bus excursion. Someone identified these women a long time ago, allowing some townsfolk to see great-grandmothers and great-aunts who they had never seen before. (D of I records.)

WEDDING OF MARGE AND MARTIN WEIR. Marge (née Schulte) and Martin Weir stand for their wedding portrait at a studio in Ubly. They were married at Our Lady of Lake Huron Catholic Church in Marge's hometown of Harbor Beach on June 9, 1945. The couple had managed to save World War II gas rations and honeymooned at their deer hunting camp in Mio. Marge died in 1966 and Martin in 2003. (Courtesy of Bob Weir.)

A DOUBLE WEDDING. Madeline "Mid" Kennedy married Joseph Keegan (both on right) and Florence Kennedy married James Keegan (both on left) in a double wedding in Our Lady of Mt. Carmel Church on September 15, 1936. They were each other's maid of honor and best man, since the women were sisters and the men were brothers. Notice how modern the ladies' shoes look. (Courtesy of Colene Keegan Pardo.)

KENNEDY-JOHNSON WEDDING. Mary Eileen Kennedy married Richard Johnson at Our Lady of Mt. Carmel. Her maid of honor was her sister Mid, and Richard's best man was his brother Roy. The Johnsons were farmers, owned a business in town, and were hay growers and transporters. All of the kids did their share of the work and it was said that the Johnson girls could throw a bale as well as any man. (Courtesy of Colene Keegan Pardo.)

PURTELL-BRENNAN WEDDING. Pictured here are, from left to right, bridesmaid Jean Kroner, maid of honor Rita Jackson, Rita Purtell, Tom Brennan, and best man Clare Haley. (Courtesy of the author.)

SHARPE WEDDING. Mary and Jim Sharpe were married at Our Lady of Mt. Carmel like so many others. They are the creators of the Sharpe clan in Emmett, many of whom still reside in or around the township. Geneva and John Sharpe and their family lived on Bricker, about a half-mile from the cemetery. Geneva still resides there. (Courtesy of Kate McClelland.)

ESCHKER-BRENNAN WEDDING. Lucille Brennan married George Eschker in Our Lady of Mt. Carmel Church. Her maid of honor was her sister Donna and his best man was his brother Frank. George was a farm worker on Lucille's parents farm. They saw each other every day, and soon announced that they would be getting married. It was about a year later that Lucille's sister Donna met Walt Francek, and soon they announced they would marry. Walt also worked for the Brennans. Finally, the parents, Jim and Ann Brennan, protested saying they were sick of their daughters marrying the employees. They were constantly looking for help. When the family gets together, mentioning this always brings a laugh. (Courtesy of Mary Jane Eschker Click.)

FRANCEK-BRENNAN WEDDING. Adolph Francek married Rosemary Hyde at Our Lady of Mt. Carmel. Her maid of honor was Lucillle Brennan and his best man was his brother John. The couple lived in Detroit but would come out to the farm to visit Rose and Albert Brennan, Rosemary's adopted parents. The Franceks had lots of boys, making it easy to get two teams together for a baseball game. (Courtesy of Mary Jane Eschker Click.)

HELINA AND HILARY LaMAY. The parents of Dan LaMay, Helina and Hilary lived in Emmett while their children were growing up. Dan LaMay and his wife, Helen Quain LaMay, live on Brandon Road, the same street Dan lived on as a child. (Courtesy of Dan and Helen LaMay.)

MACKEY-SMITH WEDDING. Alfred Mackey married Margaret Smith at Our Lady of Mt. Carmel. The couple had nine children—seven girls and two boys. One of the boys died in infancy. Notice Margaret's fine gossamer-like veil. (Courtesy of Beth and Dick Pierce.)

PIERCE-BUTLER WEDDING. Phil Pierce married Marie Butler (on left) on Thanksgiving, November 27, 1928, at Our Lady of Mt. Carmel. Gert Butler and Gus Pierce (on right) were their attendants. Her parents, John Butler and Dora Judge Butler, hosted a dinner at their home for the wedding party and a few relatives. The couple honeymooned in Chicago. (Courtesy of Maggi and Jack Kinney.)

GARRY DONNELLON AND ANN KEOUGH WEDDING. The couple was married at Our Lady of Mt. Carmel and lived on Main Street in the village of Emmett all their lives. With the help of Gramma Keough, they raised a number of children in that house, including the current St. Clair County sheriff, Tim Donnellon. The house had high ceilings, beautiful wood doors, and intricate molding. (Courtesy of the Garry Donnellon.)

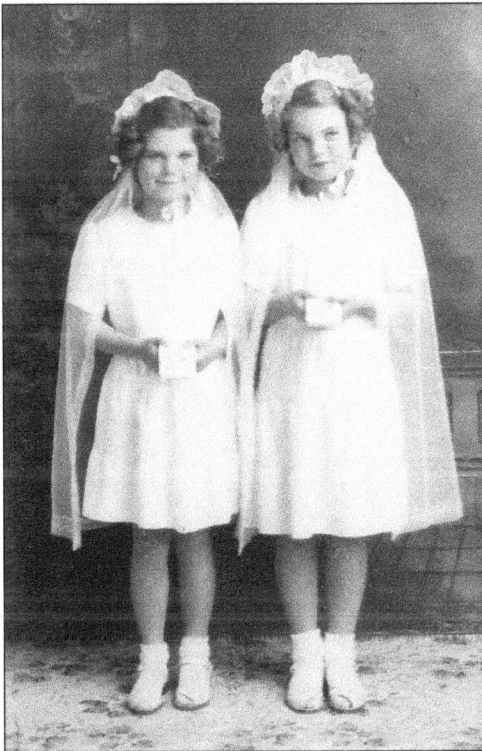

COMMUNION GIRLS. Kay and Lou Quain are the daughters of Jim and Catherine O'Connor Quain. Since this photograph was taken, they have both had children of their own who made their first communion at Our Lady of Mt. Carmel. Kay was an Emmett resident for a good portion of her life and Lou remained in Emmett, on Burt Road, where she raised her children. Her closest neighbors are Jim and Jack Cowhy. (Courtesy of Eleanor Butler.)

BASIL BUTLER AND ELEANOR QUAIN WEDDING. This handsome couple was married at Our Lady of Mt. Carmel. The beautiful train on Eleanor's dress was in style at that time. Basil Butler is one of seven Butler boys and two Butler girls. (Courtesy of Eleanor Butler.)

JOE GRACE AND MARY KEOUGH WEDDING. This couple was married at Our Lady of Mt. Carmel. Attendants, from left to right, are Jack McCabe, Mike Donahue, Garry Donnellon, best man Pat Grace, Joe Grace, Mary Keough Grace, maid of honor Ann Keough Donellon, Rosalin Simko, Helen Wendling, and Mary Quaine Grace. Joe and his brother Pat were partners in the business started by their father, Peter J. Grace Realty, across from the new bank on Main Street. (Courtesy of Mary Alice Grace.)

FIRST COMMUNION. These two pretty girls, unknown members of the Pierce-Butler family and possibly sisters, are all dressed up for first communion. Most likely, these beautiful dresses were handmade at home or in a dress shop. The picture was taken by Friesleber, located at 3932 State Street in Chicago. (Courtesy of Maggi and Jack Kinney.)

VINTAGE FIRST COMMUNION. This young lady, a member of the Reid-Crowley-Wendling family, is also ready for her first communion. This photograph, as well as the one above, holds wonderful historical value, chronicling the beautiful dresses of the time. (Courtesy of Helen Wendling.)

KENNEDY FIRST COMMUNION. From left to right, sisters Florence, Eileen, and Madeline "Mid" Kennedy are all ready for their first communion. (Courtesy of Colene Pardo.)

Our Lady Of Mt. Carmel
Emmett, Michigan
1991

ANOTHER BIG CHURCH. This drawing was done by architect Richard Cogley. The Cogleys were originally from Emmett. After another church burned, the people opted for steel instead of wood for the next church building. (Our Lady of Mt. Carmel records.)

The Reverend Jasper F. Sirianni
BORN: August 14, 1920
DIED: May 20, 2008

FR. JOHN F. FARRELL, FR. JASPER SIRIANNI. Father Farrell was pastor of Our Lady of Mt. Carmel Parish for 40 years. He was loved by all and was just learning to appreciate his retirement and relax when his church burned. Father Sirianni came to Our Lady of Mount Carmel on June 15, 1981, and remained as pastor until 2001. He retired that year but stayed on as administrator until 2005, when he left the parish to stay with friends. (Courtesy of the author.)

Fr. Thomas A. Mullally, SVD

FRS. JIM KEAN, THOMAS MULLALLY, THOMAS KUEHNEMUND. Father Kean and Father Mullally are both hometown boys and people are very supportive of them and very proud to say they are from the parish. Father Kean is currently pastor at St. Damien Parish in Pontiac, Michigan, and Father Mullally is pastor of Sacred Heart Parish in Greenville, Mississippi. Emmett's new pastor, Fr. Thomas Kuehnemund, or "Father Tom," has only recently been assigned to the parish. He has a good sense of humor; when asked for a picture for this book, he stated that he did not have one. (Our Lady of Mt. Carmel records.)

JIM KEAN AND MOTHER TERESA. Before Jim Kean became a priest at the Archdiocese of Detroit, he journeyed to India to help with the poor in Calcutta. While there, he met and worked with Mother Teresa, pictured here with Jim.

Four

Our Houses

Thomas Quain Farmhouse. This house is a good example of the Greek Revival style, with its two boxy shapes and generous front porch. It presents its gable end to the road and is painted white. Many houses in and around Emmett Township look a great deal like this one. (Courtesy of Eleanor Butler.)

JOHNSON HOME. John Johnson lived in this interesting house on Cogley Road. It has a spacious front porch and another on the second floor. Built on the side of the house, a round structure is visible. This room is called a circular and the roof looks like a little hat on top. Diane and Chuck Wood own the house today. (Courtesy of Rose Palmateer.)

O'BRIEN HOME. Earl and Clara O'Brien owned and lived in another boxy white clapboard house showing its gable end to the road. Nell Quain was Clara's mother, and she inherited the farm from her parents. It was eventually handed down to Clara and Earl. (Courtesy of Kate and Barb Cone.)

FOLEY-BUTLER-KAVANAGH. This is a beautiful redbrick house on Foley Road, originally owned by Jim and Nora Foley. Basil and Eleanor Butler purchased it from the Foleys and it is now in the hands of Jack Kavanagh and Barbara Butler Kavanagh, who raised lots of babies in that house. (Courtesy of Eleanor Butler.)

BRANDON HOME. There were seven Brandon children who lived here: Frances, Irene, Martin, Chris, Michael, Jim, and Charlie. Later, Charlie and Rita Francek lived here. It cannot be seen very clearly, but this is another white farmhouse with much the same structure. (Courtesy of Rose Palmateer.)

THE JOHN KEEGAN HOUSE. The Keegan House looks sturdy and well cared for. The house sits on a big enough hill to provide good drainage and features some nice, less common touches. The porch steps descend on the corner of the porch, which makes it look just a little out of the ordinary. The clapboard siding is also a different color on the gables, which adds some interest. (Courtesy of Rose Palmateer.)

STAPLETON HOUSE, PETROLIA, CANADA. A young William J. "Bill" Stapleton stands with Matthew Stapleton in front of his residence in Petrolia, Canada. This Canadian house is much larger than the thatched-roof houses in Ireland. Although Bill Stapleton and his family, including his son, Jim Stapleton, visited Canada quite often, Matthew never did get to Emmett. (Courtesy of Jim and Darlene Stapleton.)

RYAN HOME. Joe Ryan and Rosemary Brogan Ryan live in this older house, which is still in very good shape. The house was built by Walt McCabe and later purchased by Fred and Mae Brogan. Joe and Rosemary purchased the house from her parents in 1972 and have taken very good care of it. (Courtesy of Rosemary and Joe Ryan.)

WALENTY HOME. Dan and Betty Walenty moved to Emmett about 30 years ago and took up residence on Burt Road. Dan's idea was to move from the city and get a nice piece of land to farm, but Betty ended up doing much of the farming. They bought baby chicks and had them shipped through the post office. After they bought a cow, they were ready to farm. (Courtesy of Betty Walenty.)

HYDE HOUSE. This is the home of George and Johanna Hyde on Bryce Road in Emmett Township. The house has served as a family gathering place for years after the children were grown and had children of their own. It was a place where the kids could run and play and the adults could catch up on the family gossip. The farm has been designated as a centennial farm. (Courtesy of Karen Breen-Bondi.)

PIERCE HOME IN IRELAND. When Pat, Tom, and John Pierce and their sister Mary Murphy Pierce came to America in 1880, they left some of the family behind. A few years ago, some Emmett residents went with Maggi Kinney and met her cousins while on a trip to Ireland. The little thatched house their ancestors had lived in is still there, sitting by the Irish Sea, with cattle walking peacefully along the beach. The cousins have newer houses now, but they have kept their little home by the seas. (Courtesy of Pierce Family.)

Five

PLAY BALL

AN EMMETT TEAM. Baseball was the top sport in Emmett. Some teams even had mascots like this shiny black dog. This photograph features, from left to right, (first row) George Maurey, Leo Butler, the mascot, Gerald Butler, Emmett Brogan, and Edward Butler; (second row) V. Mackley, Clarence Bethway, Harvey King, Earl Scheible, Elmer Brogan, Jack Brogan, and Charlie King. (Courtesy of Emmett Diner.)

1970 EMMETT LITTLE LEAGUE. This 1970s Little League team featured, from left to right, (first row) Jack Pierce, Dennis Pierce, and Joe Ryan; (second row) Dick Johnson, Joe Grace, Mark Cowhy, ? Stahl, and Greg Hyde; (third row) Jerry Ureel, Vito Palazzolo, Dick Brennan, Rick Scheible, and two unidentified. (Courtesy of Joe and Rosemary Ryan.)

1980 EMMETT FIRE DEPARTMENT. The fire department baseball team in 1980 included, from left to right, (first row) Pat Dunsmore, Larry Powers, Joe Francek, and Dick Pierce; (second row) Ed Johnson, Mike Golembiewski, and Mike Pierce (behind the trophy); (third row) Pat Pierce, Jack Hazelman, Dan DeVoight, Tom Cowhy, Bill Golembiewski, Roger McClelland, Frank Golembiewski, and Dennis Pierce. (Courtesy of Dennis Pierce.)

A LONG-AGO EMMETT TEAM. Listed in no particular order, some of the members of this baseball team included ? Brogan, ? Storey, Leo Sweeney, Irwin Scheible, Peter J. Grace, A. Storey, Earl Scheible, and Walt McCabe. (Courtesy of Joe and Rosemary Ryan.)

1972 CHAMPIONS EMMETT BABE RUTH LEAGUE. Pictured here on September 7, 1972, are, from left to right, (first row) Walt Bonzar and Dave Stahl; (second row) Dick Johnson, Joe Grace, Mark Cowhy, Rick Huss, and Greg Hyde; (third row) Rick Scheible, Dave Ureel, Vito Palozzola, unidentified, and Joe Ryan. Their coach, Dennis Pierce, is not pictured. (Courtesy of Dennis Pierce.)

BASEBALL, 1908. This early baseball team featured, from left to right, (first row) Elmer Brogan, ? Brandon, John Dowd, Leo Kennedy (holding the baby), two unidentified, and Howard Maurer; (second row) ? Storey, Fred Brogan, James Dewar, Clem Cogley, ? Culcher, Manley Neaton, ? LaForge, Jim Reed, and Ed Neaton. (Courtesy of Joe and Rosemary Ryan.)

MODERN BASEBALL. The 1946 Blue Water Champs included, from left to right, (first row) Bob Carson, Jerry Butler, Stew Dunsmore, Pat Grace, Bob Morgan, Tom Haley, and Vin Ryan; (second row) Joe D., Early Scheible, Basil Butler, Mike Scheible, Clarence Bethway, Pat Donahue, and Irwin Scheible. Team member Joe Ryan was not pictured. (Courtesy of Joe and Rosemary Ryan.)

Six

OUR SCHOOLS

BRANDON SCHOOL, 1921. Students at the Brandon School posed in front of the schoolhouse in 1921. They included, in no particular order, Harvey Carpenter, Raymond Donahue, Emmett Brogan, Jack Brogan, Emmett Kassane, Jack (Fr.) Sweeney, Waverly Shoe, Lela Woods, Bernadine Hyde, Madeline Kennedy, Mary Donahue, Donna McCabe, Eileen Kennedy, Stella Kassane, Veronica Donahue, Margaret McInerey, Jean Chase, Florence Kennedy, ? Woods, Emma Hyde, Martha Van, Elizabeth Kassane, Ann Kassane, teacher Mollie Reid, Lucille Harmon, Catherine Kassane, Mary Sweeney, Alice Hand; James McInerney, Frank Ryan, Fr. Furlong, Noble McCabe, Leo Kennedy, Harold Chase, John Judd, Leo Harmon, Duffy Harmon, Elmer Hand, and Bill McIntyre. (Courtesy of Helen Wendling.)

THE HYDE SCHOOL. This school was on Bryce Road in Emmett Township. Some of the students pictured include Agnes O'Leary, Loretta Driscoll, Jim Keegan, Emma Rider, Carl Sheen, Margaret Gleason, Carl Sheen, Frank Donahue, Anna Mae Keegan, Sabina Brady, Wilfred Keegan, and Joanne O'Mara. (Courtesy of Helen Wendling.)

GRADES FIVE THROUGH EIGHT, 1909. Some of the students in this school picture are May McMabe, Albert Conger, Vera Reid, May Wilson, teacher, Louis Kennedy, Irene Kissane, Coletta Kavanagh, Peg Brandon, Nora Ryan, Hazel Reeves, Walter McCabe, Goldie Dorsey, Helen Breen, Charlotte Reid, Joe Dunnigan, Jim conger, Austin Kinney, Leo Kennedy, Owen Ryan. (Courtesy of Nora Ryan Conlan.)

MOLLIE'S SCHOOL. In the early 1900s, there were many one-room schoolhouses like Mollie's School, taught by Mollie Reid (standing, far left), including the O'Connor School on Sheridan Road, the Nolan School on Bryce Road, the Foley School on Quain Road, the Cotter School on Carney Road, and Brandon and Hyde Schools. (Courtesy of Helen Wendling.)

SWEENEY BARN. Before it was a barn, the structure in the middle of the picture was the Sweeney School. Many farms had the family name on the barn at that time, as seen above. (Courtesy of Mary Ann and Pat Quain.)

UNKNOWN CHILDREN. Mollie Reid (third row, fifth from right) poses for a school picture with a group of children who look very cold. Two more early schools in the township were the McConnell School on Quain Road and a school in the village on Prospect Street. A newer Brandon School opened in the village in 1958 and closed in 1968 when schools were consolidated with the Yale Public Schools. (Courtesy of Helen Wendling.)

CLASS PORTRAIT. This photograph of the Emmett School's ninth grade class includes, from left to right, Frances O'Neill, Nellie McIntyre, Nora Ryan, Charlotte Reid, Margaret Brandon, Joe Dunigan, and Frank Kennedy. The Michigan state constitution mandated that all school districts provide an education from kindergarten through 12th grade, but the township schools could not afford this, and by 1968, they had closed their doors. (Courtesy of Nora Ryan Conlan.)

SCHOOL. John F. Farrell-Emmett Elementary School on M-19 was built by the people of Our Lady of Mt. Carmel Parish. The cost of upkeep and difficulty hiring nuns made operation of the school impossible, and the parish sold the school to the Yale Public School System in 1974. (Courtesy of author.)

MORE UNKNOWN. Schoolrooms in the early days were packed with children. This image includes more than 50 students in one room—a large group for just one teacher to handle. (Courtesy of Helen Wendling.)

Seven

Our People

MICHAEL REID. Michael Reid, pictured here, married Margaret Crowley. They are the parents of Tom Reid, the grandparents of Helen Wendling, and the great-grandparents of Michael Wendling, the prosecuting attorney of St. Clair County. Michael and his wife, Michelle, have four children: Sean, Matt, Thomas, and Riley; they are the great-great grandchildren of Michael Reid and Margaret Crowley. (Courtesy of Helen Wendling.)

MIKE BREEN. One of the Breen family that was important in the early history of Emmett, Mike Breen is seen here. The Breens and the Brennans have crossed paths several times over the years. (Courtesy of the author.)

MICHAEL KENNEDY. In this photographic portrait, a well-turned-out Michael Kennedy wears a bowler and has a velvet collar on his wool coat. A member of the early Kennedy family, he may have been a cousin of Patrick "Pa" Kennedy. (Courtesy of Rose Palmateer.)

PIERCE-BUTLER RELATIVE. Arthur & Philbric Photographers, at 204 and 206 Woodward Avenue in Detroit, captured this image of a fine lady with a broach pin on her collar, an unusual hat, a fur wrap, and gloves. A member of the Pierce-Butler family, her name is unknown. (Courtesy of Maggie and Jack Kinney.)

COADY-PALMER FAMILY. This young member of the Coady-Palmer family looks very proper with his suit and tie. He looks ready to take on the day. (Courtesy of Elaine Rawlins.)

FR. JAMES STAPLETON. Pictured here is Fr. James Stapleton, cousin of Jim Stapleton of Stapleton Road. The family members were early settlers and obviously present for the naming of roads. Their ancestors were from the town of Nennah in the County Tipperary, Ireland. (Courtesy of Jim and Darlene Stapleton.)

IRENE BRANDON KENNEDY. In this photograph, Irene Brandon Kennedy wears a white dress without lace or embellishment, and no jewelry. But she does wear black stockings and looks neat with no frills. (Courtesy of Rose Palmateer.)

MOLLIE CROWLEY REID. Mrs. Reid was known to be a good teacher who was strict but fair. She was married to Tom Reid and their daughter is Helen Wendling. (Courtesy of Helen Wendling.)

MAUDE STAPLETON. The wife of Bill and mother of Jim Stapleton, Maude hosted her share of card parties for her lady friends in later years when she lived with Jim and Darlene. (Courtesy of Jim and Darlene Stapleton.)

FINE FASHION. This young lady is unidentified but fashionably dressed. The bodice of her dress and the long sleeves are of a lightweight patterned material, while the skirt is of a heavier material and matches the collar. The fashion of those days was a high neckline like this one. Finishing her look is a white embroidered scarf tied in a bow and a bow in her hair. (Courtesy of Maggi and Jack Kinney.)

PIERCE-BUTLER FAMILY. This Butler-Pierce relative sports the popular mustache and wears a cravat. This photography company had a lot to say on their sign before the customer could even get through the door, "Holcombe and Metzen Photographers, We have everything in the line of modern photography. Duplicates and enlargements from this negative at reduced rates, Telephone 1162." (Courtesy of the Butler/Pierce collection.)

80

M. McIntyre. A Butler-Pierce relative, this young lady could be a bride. Identified only as M. McIntyre, she wears an airy white dress and a matching hat. She also wears long white gloves, a pedant locket, and tiny white shoes. (Courtesy of the Butler/Pierce collection.)

Tailored Dress. This woman's dress was made by an excellent seamstress. The material was cut on a bias to form panels that when sewn together formed a skirt which flares out at the bottom, making the waist look smaller. The dress fits her so well; it was definitely made for her. (Courtesy of the Butler/Pierce collection.)

NEW FASHION. This stylish woman exemplified the new hairstyle of the time. She has mutton sleeves on her dress and the usual high collar with attached scarf tied in a bow. (Courtesy of Butler/Pierce collection.)

MARY WALSH BRANDON. Mary Brandon wears a black dress with a high collar and a pretty broach. As was the custom at the time, the jewelry may have been handed down from mother to daughter for generations. (Courtesy of Colene Pardo.)

JEREMIAH FOLEY. The Foleys came from Ireland like so many other families: one or two at a time when boat passage could be afforded. The relatives here in America sent what money they could, and eventually the families would reunite. (Courtesy of Mary Alice Grace.)

PETER JAMES GRACE. Seen here in his pinstripe suit, Peter Grace was an energetic man who was not afraid to venture into something new. In a land of farmers, he opened a real estate office, which included his two sons, Pat and Joe, and the business was lucrative enough to support three families. (Courtesy of Mary Alice Grace.)

OUT JOB HUNTING. This clean-cut young man with his hair parted down the middle sits for an early portrait. His suit looks like a tweed material with a light patterned shirt and tie. (Courtesy of Elaine Rawlins.)

JOHN BRENNAN. With soulful eyes and a lot of hair, John Brennan is dressed in a contemporary style with a patterned shirt and a coordinating patterned tie, a look very much in tune with today's attire. (Courtesy of Sue and Tom Barr.)

MEN'S FASHION. This man wears the ever-popular vest and cradles a fine-looking bowler hat in his arm. This photograph was taken by Eisenhardts Eagle Gallery, at 10 and 12 Michigan Avenue in Detroit. (Courtesy of Elaine Rawlins.)

BRIDGETT KEEGAN. Although there were plenty of excellent seamstresses in Emmett, Bridgett Keegan's ability to create stylish attire is clear in this wedding dress she made herself. She has an eye for the unusual pattern to set a dress apart from others, such as the bands of ruching in several areas. Dressmaking was painstaking work at the time she was doing it. (Courtesy of Rose Palmateer.)

IRENE KINNEY GRACE. A lifelong Emmett resident, Irene had two sons, Pat and Joe, with her husband, Peter James Grace. She was always there for her grandchildren, living only a few houses down. Irene could speak her mind, but a person always knew how he or she stood with her. (Courtesy of Mary Alice Grace.)

DRESSED IN LACE. This young girl exemplifies the formal wear of the period with a beautiful white lace dress and matching hat. (Courtesy of Maggi and Jack Kinney.)

ELLEN NELLIE BUTLER. This is most likely a photograph of Ellen Butler, although her family cannot confirm it with certainty. People of this time did not write names on their photographs, even when professionally taken. They probably never expected their children or their grandchildren to be so interested in their family tree. (Courtesy of Mary Alice Grace.)

CLARA KELLEY. With her hair done up in a chignon and wearing a simple necklace, young Clara Kelley strikes a charming, demure pose. (Courtesy of Eleanor Butler.)

MARY ELLEN NEATON PURTELL. Called Nellie by her friends, Mary Ellen Purtell was a quiet, patient, and kind soul who had a dry sense of humor and could hold her own with her five brothers. She married lumberman John Purtell and had a daughter, Rita. (Courtesy of the author.)

IRENE KINNEY GRACE. Irene was about 20 years old in this photograph from the 1920s. (Courtesy of Mary Alice Grace.)

CHRISTOPHER AND GERTRUDE BRANDON. When they came to Emmett, Christopher and Gertrude Brandon had two feather ticks (like a blanket but better), two feather pillows, and six geese given to her by her mother. This is the same couple who ventured into Michigan's unforgiving north woods to be a foreman and a cook. The baby's name is John. (Courtesy of Eleanor Butler.)

GRAMMA FOLEY. When Elizabeth Perkinson came from Ireland through Ellis Island, her ride did not show so she improvised and slept all night at the Statue of Liberty. They came to get her the next day with apologies. Eventually, she married Jeremiah Foley, who had a brother named P.J. and a sister named Alice. Mary Grace and Ann Donnellon's mother, Alice Kenough, was her namesake. (Courtesy of Mary Alice Grace.)

ENGAGING WITH CAMERA. This young girl wears a pretty white lace dress with only one piece of jewelry and a huge white satin bow on her head. (Courtesy of Elaine Rawlins.)

SISTERS. The Pierce girls are all spiffed up in their finery for picture day. Margaret, called "Maggi" by her friends, is married to Jack Kinney and they live in Emmett. She is the one on the stool. Edna, on the left, is married to Roy Bartlett, and Roseann, on the right, is married to John Malloy. (Courtesy of Jack and Maggi Kinney.)

PIERCE-BUTLER FAMILY. This baby girl from the Pierce-Butler family dressed up in a pretty white dress with ruffles and black boots to get her picture taken by Matousik Photographers of Chicago. (Courtesy of Jack and Maggi Kinney.)

PIERCE CHILDREN. Siblings Tim (left) and Tracey Pierce and their cousin, Pat, don their St. Patrick's Day sweaters for the parade in Port Huron. Dick Pierce and Beth Wood Pierce are Tim and Tracey's parents. Pat's parents are Dennis Pierce and Sue Wood Pierce. (Courtesy of Jack and Maggi Kinney.)

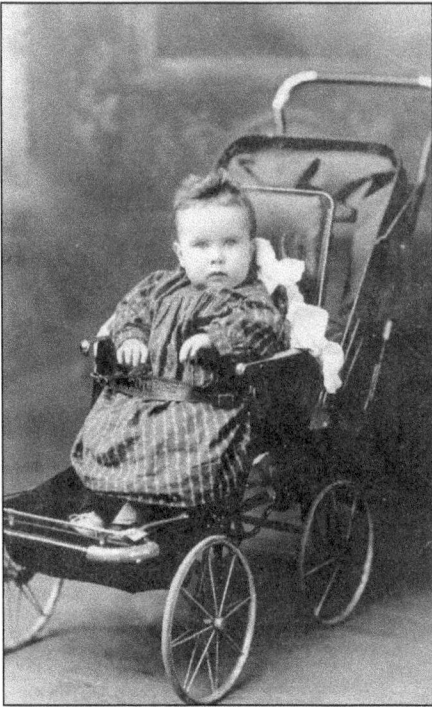

PIERCE-BUTLER FAMILY. This state-of-the-art baby carriage holds a Pierce-Butler baby in a nice patterned dress. (Courtesy of Elaine Rawlins.)

BREEN GIRLS, 1904. These two little cherubs are Mary Alma Donahue Breen (November 28, 1898–November, 10, 1982) and Kathryne Norma Donahue Craddock (December, 23, 1902–February 2, 2001). (Courtesy of Marie Therese Breen Fox.)

OUT FOR A WALK. John Crowley and Mary Ann O'Connor Crowley, the grandparents of Helen Wendling, go out for a walk on what looks like a nice summer day. (Courtesy of Helen Wendling.)

MR. AND MRS. BREEN. Dan Breen follows the fashion of the day with a vest under his suitcoat, and Mrs. Breen wears a beautifully tailored dress with a wide belt and a large silver buckle around her tiny waist. She also wears classy, understated jewelry. (Courtesy of Karen Breen-Bondi.)

O'CONNOR SISTERS. Sisters Mary Anne (left) and Anna O'Connor strike a pose together, holding roses and wearing high-necked dresses with white lace shawls. (Courtesy of Eleanor Butler.)

BRENNAN-BREEN WEDDING. In another Brennan-Breen marriage, John F. Brennan and Kathryn were married in Our Lady of Mt. Carmel Church, just as everybody in town used to be. John wears a patterned shirt and tie, and Kathryn wears a stripped dress with a sailor collar and a small broach at her neck. (Courtesy of the author.)

Tom Reid and "Uncle Ed" Crowley.
Tom Reid and "Uncle Ed" Crowley
wear extra-warm, long winter dress
coats. Tom's coat is wool with a velvet
collar and "Uncle Ed" wears a fur
coat. (Courtesy of Helen Wendling.)

Returning Soldier. Jim Burgess
is home on his first furlough.
This is Jim and his mom, Pearl.
Jim and his wife, Veronica, live
on Bricker Road. (Courtesy of
Jim and Veronica Bugess.)

KEEGAN BROTHERS. Dapper Irish brothers Joe and Jim Keegan, wearing long wool overcoats and vests, pose jokingly with their car doors still open behind them. (Courtesy of Colene Pardo.)

CHARLIE BRANDON AND TOM RAMSEY. After these two retired from farming, they would come into town, have coffee at the restaurant, and stay all day. (Courtesy of Elaine Rawlins.)

FATHER AND DAUGHTER. Michael Brandon poses with his grown daughter, Frances "Hance" Brandon in this portrait. Hance was a great friend of Eileen Johnson's and the Johnson children were especially fond of her. One or two of them were always on loan to Hance to help with her garden. (Courtesy of Rose Palmateer.)

PATRICK AND MARY MURPHY COGLEY. Patrick Cogley and Mary Murphy Cogley were the grandparents and great-grandparents of some of the Brennans still living in Emmett. Their picture hangs on the wall in the Burgess home because Veronica Burgess and her sister, Mary Agnes Dunsmore, are two of those Brennans. (Courtesy of Jim and Veronica Burgess.)

PATRICK AND BRIDGET FOGARTY BRENNAN. Patrick Brennan wears the popular vest and a complicated-looking watch fob, while his wife, Bridget Fogarty Brennan, wears a dress with a shiny muted stripe and a plaid bow at the neck. The Brennans had 13 children, beginning the family tree for all the Brennans in Emmett. (Courtesy of the author.)

BRANDON CHILDREN. From left to right, Frances, James, and Irene Brandon pose for a photograph with their dog, Trixie. Frances and Irene are pretty little girls with their hair done up and their best dresses on. James is a fine-looking young fellow, very sober and businesslike. (Courtesy of Rose Palmateer.)

THE STAPLETON
CLAN. Stapletons sit
around under one
of the big beautiful
shade trees in their
yard as is their custom
in the summer when
family members
or neighbors visit.
(Courtesy of Jim and
Darlene Stapleton.)

BUDDIES. Bill Hyde, Leo Sweeney, Fred
Brogan, and Ross McCabe had this
great photograph taken of themselves.
Notice all the different head gear. The
guys now mostly wear baseball caps.
(Courtesy of Rosemary and Joe Ryan.)

99

FOUR IN A ROW. Three guys and a girl pose for a photograph outdoors, presumably after doing some housework. They look like they could be father and sons or brothers. (Courtesy of Eleanor Butler.)

GEORGE AND JOHANNA HYDE. The Hydes owned a house on Bryce Road in Emmett Township. That house has served as a family gathering place for years after the children were grown and had children of their own. It was a place where the kids could run and play and the adults could catch up on the family gossip. The farm has been designated as a centennial farm. The Jim and Darlene Stapleton house on Stapleton Road and the Our Lady of Mr. Carmel rectory also have that distinction. (Courtesy of Jack and Maggi Kinney.)

YOUNG COUPLE. Francis Irwin Scheible and Mary Margaret Brennan married on September 5, 1914. Mary Margaret reportedly hated this picture because she was having a "bad hair day." (Courtesy of Madeline and Leo O'Connor.)

FRANK AND CARRIE MAHER BRENNAN. Frank Brennan and Carrie Maher Brennan are the parents of Thomas M. Brennan and the grandparents of Barb, Kathy, Joan, and Debbie Brennan. (Courtesy of Tom and Mary Brennan.)

ON FURLOUGH. A man welcomes a soldier back to town in this unidentified photograph. (Courtesy of Emmett Diner.)

OUTDOOR WORK. This photograph captures the day-to-day life of Emmett residents. This unidentified couple looks like the typical young couple. He is probably heading to the fields and she to the chicken coup to gather eggs. (Courtesy of Eleanor Butler.)

THE HAT. Isabell O'Connor Breen is dressed "to the nines" in this 1910 photograph. Her hat is spectacular and her dress has beautiful beading on the high neck, collar, and shoulders. This might be a wedding or an anniversary because she has a corsage and husband Henry has a boutonniere. (Courtesy of Karen Breen-Bondi.)

FOUR GENERATIONS OF FOGARTY AND BRENNAN WOMEN. Little Mary Alma Donahue Breen, age five, represents the fourth generation of Fogarty and Brennan women. She stands in front of Katherine Brennan (left), age 56; Cecilia Cogley Donahue (center), age 33; and Bridget Fogarty Brennan (right), age 82. (Courtesy of Karen Breen-Bondi.)

SURPRISE PARTY. This photograph was taken at a surprise party for Mary Grace given by the Daughters of Isabella. Women of all ages were present, from toddlers to the very old. (Courtesy of Mary Alice Grace.)

A TRIP. Evert Haley, George Mackey, Harold Brennan, and Charley McKinney took a trip out west and decided to bring back a cactus. (Courtesy of the Emmett Diner.)

PIERCE FAMILY. Pat Pierce, his wife, Ellen Jane Mackey Pierce, and their five boys pose for this family photograph. The boys are, clockwise starting at the left, Pat, Mike, Dick, Dennis, and Jack. (Courtesy of Beth and Dick Pierce.)

THE O'CONNORS. James O'Connor and Mary Wood O'Connor pose in the snow in front of their new car, a 1921 Ford Model T. They are dressed for "touring." (Courtesy of Madeline and Leo O'Connor.)

ANNIVERSARY PHOTOGRAPH. This anniversary photograph of Jack and Pearl Burgess is mounted on wood with a thin gold frame covered with laminate—a good way to preserve a photograph. (Courtesy of Jim and Veronica Burgess.)

PIERCE FAMILY. They were immigrants from Ireland in 1880. Tom, John, and Pat Pierce and Mary Pierce Murphy pose for this picture in the yard. (Courtesy of Maggi and Jack Kinney.)

STAPLETON FAMILY. Everyone is dressed in their Sunday best in this photograph. Seated, from left to right, are Kate, Agnes, Mathew (father), Mary, Margaret Gleason Stapleton (mother), and John. Standing, from left to right, are Bridget, James, Margaret, Steve, Anne, and Alice. They are all ancestors of Jim Stapleton. The women have fancy finishing touches like lace and ruching and the men all wear suits and shirts with starched collars—one even has a bow tie. (Courtesy of Jim and Darlene Stapleton.)

BOAT RIDE. Nellie Nolan, Grace Rose, Charlie Campbell, and Frank Neaton go out for a boat ride, maybe at a carnival. This foursome lived in the same area and were friends for a long time. (Courtesy of the author.)

HOMECOMING. At Emmett's 1973 homecoming, (from left to right) Martha Keegan and Lucille are in the front row and Anna May Keegan, Esther Karrigan, Nora Ryan, May Conley stand in the back row as the women pose for a photograph at Our Lady of Mr. Carmel's homecoming festivities. (Courtesy of Nora Ryan Conlan.)

THE RYANS. Pictured here are Joe Ryan's parents, Dan Ryan and Ella Clifford Ryan. (Courtesy of Joe and Rosemary Ryan.)

THE BUTLER FAMILY. The Butler siblings are all grown up in this photograph. From left to right are (seated) Basil and Vincent; (standing) Rita Carson, Elizabeth Gleason, Tom, Gerald, Ed, John, and Leo. Notice that Leo looks younger than his siblings. He was killed in World War II. The family had a picture of Leo added to this family photograph. (Courtesy of Sue and Tom Barr.)

PAT PIERCE. This is the first of many Pat Pierces in Emmett. He came to Emmett from County Wexford, Ireland. (Courtesy of Maggi and Jack Kinney.)

ED BUTLER. Ed Butler was the father of the seven boys and two girls in the Butler clan. (Courtesy of Emmett Diner.)

ALICE FOLEY KEOUGH. Alice Foley Keough was 93 years old when this picture was taken in August 1981. She was the mother of Ann Donnellon and Mary Grace and the grandmother of many. (Courtesy of Mary Alice Grace.)

ELLEN KEOUGH BUTLER.
Ed Butler's wife, Ellen
Keough Butler, raised their
brood of seven boys and
two girls. It was a very
lively household. (Courtesy
of Mary Alice Grace.)

CHUCK PIERCE. Chuck Pierce,
the brother of Mary Butler,
grew up in Emmett and still
comes back to visit occasionally.
(Courtesy of Eleanor Butler.)

JOSEPH GRACE. Joe Grace poses for a photograph in his Navy days. (Courtesy of Mary Alice Grace.)

LEO KINNEY. Raised in Emmett, Leo Kinney became an officer for the Detroit police force. (Courtesy of Mary Alice Grace.)

GERALD BUTLER. Gerald Butler was newly married when he joined the Navy to avoid the World War II draft, saying he would rather be on a boat where no one could sneak up on him. When his time was up, he collected his little girl, Sue, and his wife, Helen, in Detroit and came home to Emmett, but it was not long before they headed back to Detroit to find work, eventually making it back home to stay. (Courtesy of Sue and Tom Barr.)

HELEN BRENNAN BUTLER. Helen Brennan married Gerald Butler in 1943, and gave birth to their daughter, Sue, in 1945. With her husband fighting in the Navy, she and Sue lived in Detroit with her sister, Catherine, and her husband, Tom Flannigan. Helen got a job at Dodge Truck driving big trucks off the assembly line to a lot quite a distance away and hitchhiking back. She is the one who was "collected" after World War II, and Sue Barr is the little girl. (Courtesy of Sue and Tom Barr.)

KELLEY FAMILY. The Kelleys posed for a professional photograph with the entire family. Pictured are, from left to right, (first row) Nell Quaine, Ellen O'Brien (mother), William Kelly (father), and Genevive; (second row) Blanche Brennan, George, Bertha (Sr. Rose Vincent), Emanuel, and Clara Mackey. (Courtesy of Eleanor Butler.)

NEW POSTCARD. The town council, in conjunction with the township's elected officials, decided to have another postcard made. The ones of the town were well received, but they wanted something different. After much deliberation, they decided this reference to "crank" was the one. (Courtesy of Sally Lichota.)

EARL AND CLARA O'BRIEN. Earl and Clara O'Brien were married on October 29, 1918. Dick Brennan and Agnes O'Brien were the attendants. Clara and Earl O'Brien and Tom and Rita Brennan were great friends. Clara was Tom's aunt. (Courtesy of Kate and Barb Cone.)

BUTLER CHILDREN. These siblings look like they are going into battle with a baseball and a mitt, two bats, and two BB guns. Shown here from left to right are Lorraine and Theresa in front and are Basil, Jack, and Margaret Butler in back. (Courtesy of Ray and Vicki Gleason.)

ELIZABETH GLEASON. As Elizabeth Gleason stepped out of the car on her honeymoon in Florida in 1930, she looked like she just came from the cold of Michigan. She has on a heavy wool coat with a huge fur collar and fur on the sleeve cuffs. (Courtesy of Ray and Vicki Gleason.)

CUTE KIDS. From left to right, Tom, Helen, and Catherine—the children of John F. and Kathryn Breen Brennan—pose for a photograph. Tom, with his long curls, is the author's father. (Courtesy of Sue and Tom Barr.)

LITTLE GIRL. This young girl holds a serious expression in this formal photograph. Her dress has ruching, ruffles, and puffy sleeves. Unfortunately, there is no record of her name. (Courtesy of Mary Alice Grace.)

RITA PURTELL. Young Rita Purtell poses with a huge bow in her hair. The daughter of Mary Ellen Neaton Purtell and lumberman John Purtell, as a child she lamented how much her father was gone. (Courtesy of the author.)

SWEENEY CHILDREN. Pictured from left to right, Joseph, Alex (holding baby sister Mary Ann), Laurence, and William Sweeney smiled for the camera while on a walk. Mary Ann recalls that her brothers "hauled me with them every place they went and did not seem to mind at all." (Courtesy of Mary Ann Quain.)

IRISH COUPLES. James O'Brien (who died at the age of 94) and Ann Griffin O'Brien (who died at the age of 71) are the couple on the right. On the left are Thomas Brennan and Catherine Mackey Brennan. These two couples live a long time considering the lack of medical care at the time. (Courtesy of Kate and Barb Cone.)

A CROWD AT THE EMMETT HOTEL, 1942. This crew of friends enjoys a drink together in the afternoon. The group included (first row) Marty Ryan and Harold Ryan; (second row) James Gleason, Bill Butler, Leo Dunnigan, and Gerald Butler; (third row) Clarence Bethway, Albert Butler, Bill Morgan, and Bernie Quain. (Courtesy of Emmett Diner.)

YOUNG MEN. From left to right, Gordon Mathews, Cecil McIntosh, Cyril Nelson, and Charley Guerton look like a colorful bunch of friends. Notice the variety of attire they wear, especially the hats and vests. (Courtesy of Mary Alice Grace.)

PALMER RELATIVES. These two young women are relatives of the Palmer-Coady family. The necklines of their dresses are very high and tied up with big bows, and the bodice is corset-like. The photograph was taken by J.W. Crealy Photographers of Strathroy, Ontario, Canada. (Courtesy of Elaine Rawlins.)

JOHN PURTELL. John Purtell and his wife, Mary Ellen, only had one child, Rita, which meant it was just the girls when John was gone for long stretches at lumber camps. (Courtesy of the author.)

Two Generations. Pictured from left to right are Joe, John, and Pat Grace, owners of Peter J. Grace Realty. Both men are wearing patterned jackets and patterned ties and little John looks spiffy in his Navy sailor suit. Joe is John's dad and Pat is his uncle. (Courtesy of Mary Alice Grace.)

90th Birthday. Helen Quain (center) poses for a celebratory photograph with her son, Pat (left) and his wife, Mary Ann, on her 90th birthday. (Courtesy of the Dan and Helen Lamay.)

ANNIVERSARY. Clem and Helen Quain prepare to cut the cake at their 20th wedding anniversary in 1954. (Courtesy of Helen and Dan LaMay.)

HUNTING. From left to right, Vin Ryan, ? Gibber, Pat Grace, Basil Butler, and Vin O'Connor pose for a photograph on a deer-hunting trip. When the guys go "up north" during hunting season, everything in Michigan gets put on hold. Daughters cannot even get married during hunting season. (Courtesy of Mary Alice Grace.)

BUTLER CHILDREN. Shown from left to right, Lorraine, Margaret, Theresa, and Jack Butler piled into this cart with a sheep to pose for a photograph in 1930. (Courtesy of Ray and Vicki Gleason.)

WEDDING BREAKFAST. This picture was taken at the wedding breakfast of Mary and Pat Grace. Several guests were Emmett people, including (in no particular order) Mary Quaine Grace, Pat Grace, Father Farrell, Lucille Quaine, Brennan, Dolores Burns Quaine, Ambrose Kinney, Marion Maher Kinney, Rosemary Ryan, Mary Grace Bartolo, Ann Haley Grace, Frank Grace, Ed Grace, and Peter and Irene Grace. (Courtesy of Mary Alice Grace.)

GLEASON FAMILY. Nellie and Dan Gleason pose for a photograph in a field with their children, (left to right) James, Helen, Tom, and Catherine, and the baby is Mary Jo. (Courtesy of Ray and Vicki Gleason.)

BUTLER FAMILY. Leo Butler and his wife, Isabelle, walk with their children, Tim and Mary Pat. Leo was killed in World War II but was remembered well by the big Butler clan. This is the Butler brother the family added to the photograph on page 109. (Courtesy of Ray and Vicki Gleason.)

BREEN FAMILY PICTURE. This family photograph was taken after Dan Breen's funeral. His wife, Isabelle, sits on the far left. (Courtesy of Karen Breen-Bondi.)

WINNING BOWLING TEAM. Pictured from left to right, Alice Donnellon, Irene Grace, Rosie Burns, Wanda Lydecker, and Rita Butler Carson journeyed to Flint to participate in the Women's State Bowling Tournament in 1957. (Courtesy of Mary Alice Grace.)

MILK TRUCK. Dan Gleason hauled his milk to the creamery in Emmett in his old Model T truck. When his neighbors found out about this, they asked him to haul theirs too, and a milk route began. When the bands on his transmission were worn and could not make the hill in Memphis going forward, Gleason would back up the hill with the load of milk. He eventually bought a 1932 Model B truck and spent the rest of his working life with it. Ray still has the truck pictured here with Dan and Rita Gleason sitting on the fenders. (Courtesy of Vicki and Ray Gleason.)

COADY-PALMER RELATIVES. These unidentified Coady-Palmer relatives depict the fashion of their era. These people lived in a world of hard labor and inconvenient circumstances, but still managed to find the time to look nice on special occasions. This photograph was taken by Foote Photographer at 500 Saginaw Street in Flint. (Courtesy of Elaine Rawlins.)

THOMAS QUAIN FAMILY. On the first page of chapter 4 is a photograph of this family on the front porch of their farm house. Here is a closeup of the handsome family members after they brought chairs onto the lawn. They are ancestors of Eleanor Butler and Madeline Doherty. (Courtesy of Eleanor Butler.)

CHERRY PIE. These happy young men and women enjoy some dessert. Shown in no particular order are Bessie Nolan, Bill Cody, Alice Omara, Guy Cody, Peggy Stark, Sarah Foley, and Nellie Nolan. (Courtesy of Elaine and Don Rawlins.)

Visit us at
arcadiapublishing.com

www.ingramcontent.com/pod-product-compliance
Lightning Source LLC
Chambersburg PA
CBHW080628110426
42813CB00006B/1625